What's True About You?
Are You a Chicken Head?

Written by
Connie Witter

Illustrated by
Angel Lazio

because of Jesus
publishing

Victoria and her family went to a party one day.
She met some new children who wanted to play.

They decided to play the game

"Hide and Seek,"

so they shut their eyes and did
not peek.

One of the girls turned off the light;
the darkness gave Victoria such a terrible fright!

Her words hurt Victoria's heart;
yes, they did.
So she ran to her mom and
tearfully said,

"Tell that girl not to call me a
chicken head!"

Her Mom looked at Victoria with love in her eyes and said,

"Sweetie, there's no need to cry. Is what that girl said about you true? Are you a chicken head?

What does Jesus say about you?"

Victoria thought about what her mom had said,
then happy thoughts filled her head.

"Well, Jesus says I'm

wonderful, precious,
and special, too!"

Mom smiled and said,
"Yes, Victoria, that's what's true
about you!"

You made me amazing and wonderful. ~Psalm 139:14~

"Now, Victoria, you have a
choice, yes, you do.
Will you believe that girl, or what
Jesus says about you?"

Victoria thought for a minute, then declared with glee
"Mom, I believe what Jesus says about me!"

"That's right, Victoria, I'm so proud of you! You are wonderful, precious, and special too!

It doesn't matter what others say about you, because what Jesus says is always true!"

- - - - - - - - - - - - - -

You are a chosen race...God's own purchased, special people. ~1 Peter 2:9~

Mom looked at Victoria with a
smile on her face.
Victoria had chosen to believe Jesus
and receive His grace.

Victoria's heart was filled
with joy that day;
so, with a smile on her face
she ran off to play.

People sometimes say things that can hurt your heart, but if you'll turn to Jesus, He'll remind you of who you are!

So, next time someone says mean words to you, you can boldly say "That's not true!

I believe what Jesus says!

I am wonderful, precious and special, too;
because Jesus said it, that makes it true!"

You are precious and honored in my sight and I love you.
~Isaiah 43:4~

For additional copies of this book or for more
information on books published by
Because of Jesus Publishing,
visit us at
www.becauseofjesus.com

Text copyright © 2015 by Connie Witter
conniewitter.com
Illustrations Copyright © 2015 by Angel Lazio
alazio96@gmail.com

Published by Because of Jesus Publishing
PO Box 3064
Broken Arrow, OK 74013-3064
www.becauseofjesus.com

ISBN: 978-0-9883801-7-2

Cover and interior design: Angel Lazio